I0839269

Finding friend Goxhan Yuzsitmeek in Mountain View under Oakland

------A collection of scattered Footsteps in Poetic Forum (II)

Benny Wu
Lanfeng Yu
Lilyn Cheekawood
James Murphy
Jenny Zhang

Irene Harlequinn Publishing at Abbey Square of New York City
A Tom Doherty Associates Book In-Cooperation of British Library

Books that Benny, Lanfeng , Lilyn, James, and Jenny endorse:

Counting Songs for Young Readers By Jingle Yan
Mad Cat King IV by Annapolis Montuwa
The Frog Music at Far East Salt Well by Venetian Peng
Poems of Love and the Sea : 21 chap book by Gloria Gay
The Royal Wedding: Prince William & Kate Middleton:
A Celebration through Poetry by Moeze M. Latji
The Best Australian Poems 2013 by Lisa Gorton, Les Murray,
On Paisley Grovjaxiquzkerr Rodhamucrowfawnt, the piglet and her
older brother by Pheobe Rory-Stephanie QinGates, London WhelanMitt
Bigly: Donald Trump in Verse by Rob Long
Frice dishes at Riverside, Essays of Qingxuan Lin,
Both Move qi Yan by Ameliawood Yarisford
according to the wall street journal, Baker, Gigot by Jingle Yan
When Is The Good Time For Lawrence To Visit Salt Lake City of Utah State?:
by Thomas owen Washington, jewelry Samantha Paris
Novelty Shop by Ina Davis
Marissa Mayer and the Fight to Save Yahoo by Nicholas Carlson
Harry Potter and the Sorcerer's Stone (#1) By J. K. Rowling, Mary Grandpre
Dufossat Jinikoh bumps into Thomas Hall at Wilson Street by Trina Beck
Traps by Mackenzie Bezos
Iit takes a Village by Hilary Rodham Clinton, Marla FRazee
Less Is More, more Is Less by Nathan Brown
Steven Jobs: The Man Who Thought different by Karen Blumenthal
Grace Awakening by Shawn Bird
Shake A Leg by Constance Allen, Maggie Swanson
Dr. Tom Wu's Different Approach in Natural Healing: Conquer Cancer and
Other Diseases with Simple Foods by Tom Wu, Constance Vincent
Navier-Stokes Equations by Peter Constantin, Ciprian Foias
'poetry journal by Dartan Creations
The Rain in Portugal (poems) by Billy Collins
Barney & Friends: Christmas Star by Jim Rowley
April and Avery by Helen Wu

To Suri, Shiloh, Pax, London, Sam, Tina, Eric, Steven, Samba,
and
to April, Oliver, Thorton, Lilyn, Frank, Mary, Chris, Tom, Jane,
or
Eric, Steven, Tacy, Arzelar, Rufuz, Jerry, Marissa, Zachary, Min

to Drew, Martha, Aaron, Marissa, Meet, Markshen, Seth, Abbey

Amelia, Kathleen, Evelyn, Paula, Donovan, Malia, Sasha, Julie

some people sit in their powerful office,
making important decisions,
from ordinary professor to well known actors,
from presidents to silicon valley technology key people,
all share one thing in common: respect, honor, distance…

as a writer, we would love to mention the following for their
outstanding respect and honorable treatments to our efforts in poetry
and story writing, especially when we have a platform from

Thursday poets Rally week 86,
Sixth International nutrition Month in April, 2018

Tsai Ing-Wen
Chiang Kai-shek
Chen Chienjen
William Lai
Shih Junji
Lee Tenghui
Chen Shuibian
Ma Yingjeon
Penny Wilson
Kathy Parker
Jim Rowley
Sheryl Leah
Stephen White
Heather Smith
Sue Shinn
Tim Platt
Larry Rifkin
Dennis Deshaker
Richard Leach
Alfred Zucker
Xi Jingping
Donald Trump
Burns Hargis

for people who opt to share meals in a few Beijing attraction,
Guangzhou attraction, and Shenzhen attraction, Taipei attraction,
we seriously type their names here:

许明　Xu Ming

张双虎　Zhang Shuanghu

李敬挪　Li Jingnuo

陈更　Cheng Geng

林治武　Lin Zhiwu

夏俊雄　Xia Junxiong

李进开　Li Jingkai

董波青　Dong Boqing

徐孝精　Xu xiaojing

袁建明　Yuan Juanming

刘红霞　Liu Hongxia

杨建林　Yang Jianling

陈奕坤　Chen yikun

朱一航　Zhu Yihang

陈平炎　Chen Pingyan

韩皮龚　Han Pigong

杨桐　Yang Tong

酒泉森　Jiu quansen

郭柏灵　Guo Boling

苗长兴　miao changxin

田钢　Tian Gang

彭于晏　Peng Chuanxian

吴家宏 Wu Jiahong

严歌苓 Yan Ji

冯小刚 Feng Dequan

吴胜 Wu Sheng

樊敏 Fan Min

赵坤 Zhao Kun

伊伦静 Yi Lunjing

龚肖 Gong xiao

泛美华 Fan Meihua

管莉 guan li

朱戴方 zhu daifang

寒冰 Han Bing

王德华 Wang Dehua

孟建国 Meng Jianguo

隋玲 Sui Ling

朱超 Zhu Cao

严蓉 Yan Rong

胡玮炜 Hu Weiwei

吴文慧 Wu Wenhui

柳士和 Liu Shihe

杨之源 Yang Zhiyuan

王贵强 Wang Guiqiang

冯提莫 Feng Shui E

孙建飞 Sun Jianfei

颜彭川 Yan Pengchuan

戴望冰 Dai Wangbing

严群 yan qun

Shenzhen gateway China East air

tim Kobe
ti Mobile phone
joyvio

a couplet says:
" Shan Di Gong Yuan Sheng
 Duo Cai Gui Zhou Feng?

moutai wine
guizhou special
AQuos, Pingan bank,
Shenzhen Attraction

yichen dai
hua qiu
ruihong ji, alan noel, carson james, scott Larson, all study m.

Taipei Story Slams (shortlist)

shui hu zhuan by Gong minghong
qi qi li xian ji by Ying Pingshu
yong bao zixing ren sheng by wu tanru
Ye Ban shou tou by liu ji
you qu de wei da gu shi by xie yingchong
100 hope by Zeng Zhilang
Chuan Wai by Chiong Yao
Life memory by Lin Qingxia
Cartoon by Wanda Coven
Tom Sawyer by Mark Twain
Dairy by Jane Mendelsoh
Drama by Timothy Snyder
short verse by simon Sineka
the nickel-plated beauty by Patricia Beatty
Joshua by Joseph F. Girzone
Jeffrey and the Third –Grade Christmas visitors Ghost by Megan
Stine
Cat's Cradle by Kurt Vonnegut
Revenge of the Snob Squad by Julie Anne Peters

Mark Yakich's poetry theory

a book themed on poetry
scribbles of thoughts on possibility of molding
a startup of random things
events of their imaginary numbers
reflection of a moon
the shadow and the invisible object
which says " poetry in abstract observations"
new York, boston, san jose, pittsburg, denton, college station
or Princeton, flagstaff, baton rouge, page, Austin, Sherman,
places converge
in poetic notes
freedom and romantic expression rise in a black ball
of
hummingbirds

The bushes, hagers, welchs, pierces, Herbert's, poppy, walkers

two twin girls
they grow up at Bush's Houston Ranch
Jenna, and Barbara,
under George and Laura Bush,
the tree,
the lawn,
the horses,
 the Red River,
 one is revolted into three units,
 Margret Laura Mila, Poppy Louise Wendy, Alexia Philllips,
Henry Hager and Jena Bush are happy couples,
Jeb Bush, Zach Johnson, Leon Jones, John Nicklow, Eric Schmidt,
these distant relatives are curious
why Barbara Bush and Mary Oliver join Kay Ryan,
pushing Library Card system into London Train of J. K. Rowling,
But, pause,
until Jose Fine, Silvio Clinton, Steve Stone, Marvin Harps win,
we all sit,
patiently,
waiting for arrivals of Mr. and Ms. smith to sign their names
Beverly Hills echo Angela Jolie and Brad Pitt movements,
Bemidji of Minnesota prints Tom Cruise, Tom Hanks,
how about stop reading for a chance,
how about start writing
writing about Calvin Mays, Lucille Mays, Kathleen Wilson
in how they encounter Paul Tulane and John Audubon
and how Abigail Keegan and Mark Parker turn red light to green

Wow, CBS, Guiyang city, Yang Ji city, and Anderson Cooper

mother Gloria Venderbilt in nice
she joins her son
making Anderson Cooper a powerful news-crew
yahoo co-founder Jerry and David may not know,
but we know, as google search says,
"Sui Ling"
"Zhu Cao"
"Yang Lan"
"Tian Junxian"
"Zhen Baoxia"
"Wei Yuan"
"Xu Jianying"
"Liu Ying"
"Fan Meihua"
"Yi Kesong"
"Gong Xiao"
"Yan Qun"
"Gao Hongjian"
"Ji Shengxiong"
"Zhou Huiju"
…
Gerad Clancy and amelia zheng,
Frank wang and angela zhu,
Nick murphy and Senta wang,
Ruibo li and Lori Webster,
all have transformational movements at New York city

Grace Hsu and Peter Cooley's seashell picking

Barnes & Noble did that,
Sheryl Sandberg knows things well,
so does Jonathan Rosenburg,
their mid-west lake Michigan cruise sails far
far enough to reach rome,
making Florence, Cojitoab, Audubon, Murphy rise,
rise high enough to the Sun,
hot enough to burn Jean Lafitte swamp,

what do ya think of me?
I swing my way zig-zag,
 seeing Yan Qingzhi, Dale Alspach, Saint Francis,
 passing Yan Yizhi, Bruce Barry, Saint Abilene,
 images of Fuyi, Qianlong, Kangxi, Hanwu appear,
 ...
divine margins
all made well by Peter Cooley and Richard Huang

Quote

"Brightness falls from the air."

-------------- Thomas Nashe

Place poems somewhere inspired by Jorie Graham

place
poems
somewhere
anywhere
until
the words
inhale
into
your
lung
so
we
agree
to
digest
more
poems
later

Arishbe in Augusto & Virginia Miceli Collection

a name
a logic
a fame
a choice
that is what Juliette Peirce knows,

Arishbe
Quarry
Narrative
Errand
Susan Howe has all true voice painted dark blues

way to go
John Ashberg

Ron Rash's selective voice

Shelton laurel shall not quit
if she stops jogging at wood
the birds will not chirp
the moon may not appear,
December sky costs a fog,
constructing a snow-fever,
if I cough,
if I sneeze,
My day may be hauled by Virginia wolf,
since I sit,
absorbing obama~ trump~ yarisford~ bushhager~ clintonblythe
which makes Ron Rash as a good thing,
Brown Lung, Car Tags, Ginseng, Spear point
all turtles hit the water hard

Homegoing with Yaa Gyasi

she is strong
making her way to London
boarding a plane to Paris
we watch a movie by Tom Hanks and Elizabeth Banks
Pass a book written by Jhumpa Lahiri
when we eat Hainan meals
we remember Hope Jahren
we remember Harper Lee
we remember Gloria Gay
we remember Nepal Philippine
 we remember Constance Vincent

somewhere,
in Frankford airport,
Frank Watson, Stephan Wilson wink,
Sheila Why, Karen Baker, Todd Holm, Anne Holm tie knots
tossing some fog into our face

Myra Clare Rogers and James Mitchell Rogers

Newcomb college,
Relatives of William Penn Roger,
Tacy Stevens, Jane Garland, Jennifer Noel, Sarah Parish,
they set up good chapel
making life accessible
we recall a teaching job
at Will Roger Elementary School,
we appreciate Will Roger college,
the way we adore Tulsa community college,
the way we respect Capital Normal University,
and Will roger airport shy away in mixed stance
assuming Rice University, university of Washington
we march long
here and there
up and down
Michigan, Texas, Kansas, Arkansas, Idaho, Oregon, Utah,
Colorado, South Carolina, North Dakota, Montana, Florida

Why Daniel sharp and Rebecca Wells shall write?

He wonders
So does Brandt Dixon
But
Arynne Farnin decides to write,
so do Annapolis Montuwa, or Helen Wu,
today I visited Elaine McWilliams
feel good about continuation
of freedom
or poetic writing
through amazon, barnes & noble, ebay,
we discover Yan Geling, Mo Yan, Ha Jin, Lawrence Yep,
we become better known through
Jingle Yan, Uwe Gordon, Scott Jackson, Laura Bush

Jeff Powers, Steven Jobs, and Eric Wood telescopes

1990s ~~ 2020s, on Tulane –Loyola-Xavier-Brown-Yale,
30 years of run
cross India Ocean
Beyond Mt. Everest
None of us can predict others
Nanchang, Changsha, Wuhan, Hanyang, Hangkou, Shantou,
Guangzhou, Tianmen, Shijiazhuang, Shanghai, Shenzhen,
people zigzag through universe,
doting out a skyful stars---
facebook, Apple, Alibaba, yahoo, Pixma, Hollywood, crescent,
Microsoft, Motorola, google, twitter, facebook, youtube, Cisco,
not exclude Baidu.com, abebooks,
once all on youtube freely
we begin to drop our jaws,
since we know wu aimei, Cheng Li, Yang Meiling, Ma Bing,
we also know Tang Gangqing, Peng Chuanhui, He zhangmei,
teachers such as He Jiaying, Peng Hounian, Yan Siling, Bie Mama
all shift their positions,
redoing honor rolls with Chen Guiqiang, Zeng Xinxian, Man Zhen
making students know better about modern technology
and thus, we may or may not feel perfect,
but we always stay hopeful
praying for Yan Fei, Wang Xinzhou, Chen Jiaqing, Shuai Jialiang

Maroon " Headline" on Largest donor Maedell Hoover Braud

from Dec 8, 2017,
New Orleans,
Loyola University student news outlet,
a $10 Million donation
made according to Caleb Beck, Trina Beck,
under "Murphy ~ Rouse ~ Disney ~ Braud" scholarship
Jim Parter, Steven Ferguson, Jane Ferguson, Megan Barry,
john Henry murphy, Samantha murphy, elena murphy, dana murphy, aly buffett,
jane nicklow, anna pierce, tina wu,
interpreted the news
I trust Abbey Wood enough to continue my journey
adding Bailey Hendrickson, Sam Lux, Philip Hwang to our list,
never mind those worries of Shiloh Pitt, Suri Cruise, Emily Wu

Books

Books

Books

Books

Peggy loves books
the way she loves steamed yams
first, we rent
then, we buy
now we write
then we print
Books are for Readers

Come on
Lets Read more
Lets Make More

Emma Wilsonwood's Book Shelf 4 2018 Spring

Amazon.com or Barnes & Noble

Maia Wojciechowska
Robert Louis Stevenson
Karen Hill
Melania Trump
Laura Bush
Hilary Clinton
Michelle Obama
Maggie Swason
Helen Wu
Andrea Cheng
Anna Wang
Janet Wang
Emily Wang
Judy Blume
Barbara Park
Laura Ingalls Wilder
John James Audubon
Marc Brown
Mary Pope Osborne
Jack Patton
Jingle Yan
Yiling Erin Zuo
Venetian Peng
Jackie Chan
Wilson Gremer

Angela Zhu
Annapolis Montuwa
Sarah Thorrick
Malia Obama
Sasha Obama
Christina Fallin
Jay Williams & Raymond Abrashkin
John Loeper
Johanna Johnston
Jim Murphy
David Smith
Maxine Hong Kingston
Doug Cushman
Bethany Roberts
Jingle Peng
Anne Davis Peence
Sara Taylor
Jake Hargis
Peter Constantin
Don Belt
Scott Larson
Carson James
David Paige
Wendy James
Lily Milwit
Jing Wang
Bob Young
Jeff Bezos
Morton Schapiro

Bunkie, Omaha, Dangerfield, Marshall, Lena Texas 49 /259

a good stop
 exxon, shell, murphy usa, seven-eleven, clark, Anderson,
Marshall of Texas Wafflers
Comfort Inn
 Denton Vile,
 all know New Orleans / Penn Yan quite well

The Band Keeper --- > Japanese Names

Blind curtains
Music brings up light
Heart string fine tuned
Relations Blossomed

Horned by Seji Kata girl
Conducted by Wakaba Nogmute
 audience increased
 confidence rises

Koyoji Miyamoto improves the sound
Chatter, Laughter, Footsteps,
Princeton Policemen arrested into the program list
more readers nap at lots of dreamy words

Fa Yi Xuan food, Jiu Xinyi, Jiu Yuxi, Xing Mei,
Kaiyu Sheyuma, Yulong international hotel
markshen donaldwood vs frank seth shengbutow
little boy is curious about outcome of our playful lines

Jinlong Tan, Merriam Webster

薛理勇, she cares
a red sugar tea
a hot ginger soup
 that cures

九域西, 金新月,
two girls
yulong fuyi xuan food sampler
all eat well

杨万荣, 应力,
 half way guts between rome and berlin
 Xie Liyong, Wang wuquan, Yang Guoping, wang Jiuzhi,
 they forgive Yang Qingming, Hu Songzhi, Lee Fan, Peng Yuan

 一棵松, 龚晓,
 a pinewood and a morning rooster
 they form a lovely view in dawn
 Seth and Markshen seem okay with Tom and andy

Laurence Oliver's Oscar Award to Hu Xiao shan Zhuang

he performs
joan Plowwright, Vivien Leigh, Jill Esmond,
they watch,
 closely

ever since he was born
1907, may 22,
(grand parents 1688, January 11, as Jessica Hsuan, Joseph Msam)
he has records on Walt Disney

1989, july 11,
 Sussex, Steyning
 One of the Giant Stars,
 or "Thai Dou" 泰斗

 now, we recall Elizabeth Jacobsen
"Knight" "Life Peter" "Princess Lilyn"
 or Jueshi, Zhongshengguichou, Gongzhu Jinks
 what surprise to Laurence Kerr Oliver

 Sashi Biya, William shakespears,
 Charles Bennett, Chalishi Baijuyi
 directed lots of movies, " Q planes"
 saying, "Westwood Passage" "Wuthering Heights"

Zhang Xinwei, Chen Shigang, Guo boling, Xi Jingping

they reside on Dimeng hotel
shopping at Cuiwei store
Cooking Ginger soup at Mudan Garden
when Wu Jiahong and Miao Changxin give a lecture,
attracting audiences
Zhang Zhifei, Sun JiGuang, Yin Zhiping, Hu Xuefeng,
Qing Mingpu, Liu Yu, Tao Ningpu, Zheng Fawei,
 all take notes,
having fun at Jiu Suo, applied math research center
yuan jia, zhu ciqi, wang yanzhen, su hui, yan ji, all seem okay

tulane's bricktown

mark brown
derby brown
they milk cows

when gary soto and robin Perini introduce Apple orchard,
Brad Henry and Kimberly Henry change their mind
Laura Watts waves a basket for Sean Bedraza

If I decide to buy a ocean spray,
I meant to influence laura, tayre, anne, paisley, sheby, and abby
what is the reason you ignore Harvard Drew?

a unique birthday

1/12/2018
Prince Thorton was born
Barns 7 Noble celebrity,
to Xi / Peng,
He is "Hong Bao Yu Lu Bu"
to Trump / Pence
He is Eric Hill
a famous puppy for Helen Wu, Olivia Kong,
Meredith University pins a pony tail,
trying to please some piglets,
"oink" "oink"
the puppy sounds odd,
teasing Xin Yu, Sabine Schmidtle, Ari Wood, Scott Pippen,
I understand, that,
nothing is wrong,
despite that Markshen Wu is caught between "oxen and Mouse pad"
the truth is,
he is a fresh hair in the den of Central Park at New York city,
a proud thing: prince Thorton walks within 50 days

Princeton IAS: Russian is in favor of Rashid Sunyaev

 old Putin styles
He has a coin for Rashid Sunyaev,
empowering Adrian Hamers,
who has become a better Moscow space swimmer,
so, Mike and anne Greenwood plays tennis well,
Sherman Smith and Thomas Boone Pickens throw a ball
it flies cross Ellis Ye Yuan,
all math/economic students vote Yes on
Julie Cordova, Avi Wigderson, Ning Ju, Hu Weiwei, Pat Gay

Coffee Waves

Jack in the Box
Caribou
WhatABurger
Daylight Donut
Diet Coke
Starbucks
Oncue
Braum's
McCafe
BK Joe
Costa
Redhead Roasters
Red Rock
Apsen
Burger King
Canes
Five Guys
Tom's
Green Dot's
Page & Page's
Yaya's Kitchen
Jimmy's Egg
Mcdonald's
PJ's

who is 彭川惠普? who is Peng chuan hui?

who is pengchuan huipu?
who is yinge yanwu?

Wu Tianfagn   (grand grand father)
            (Zhou Baokui)

Wu Huilan   Tang Xiangyang
Wu Xitang   **Peng Tianliang**

Tang Xian   Qian Yu
Peng Zhongqiang Zhang Hong

V
V

Tang Jiezhong,   Guo xiaochuan
Peng Shuisheng Yuan Huiqing
Peng Gaoyan   Tong Simei
Peng Keqiang   Huang xiaomin

V
V

Tang Gangqing   Xu Bo
Tang Gangbo   Yang Lan
Tang Gangbiao   Zhu Ai E
Tang Qinghua   Michael Dell

Peng Chuanbing   (Brad Henry)
Peng Chuanjun   (Sophia Bollag)
Peng rongrong   (Derby Brown)

Peng Chuanhui   (Rachel Coterrill)
Peng Chuanxian   (Mark Turner)
Peng Chuanzhen   (Melania Trump)

V
V

Malia Obama
Sasha Obama
Xu xiaojing
Xu Lingxia
Xu xiangyang
Xu Bo Tang Gangqing
Leo Ku   Yongqi Liang
Pheobe Gates

ann blair
joseph singer
janet ruscher
rory Gates
Jennifer Gates
alexa dell
spencer dell
Zachary dell
laynie henry
Baylee henry
leah henry
Li guan
Tarye Brown
Laura Brown
Jennifer Brown
Maybelle Bollag Noel
Samba Noel
Sheng Wu
Tom Lee Wu
Moonie Turner
Python turner
June Turner
Jack Turner
Ying Liu
Steven Trump
Eric Trump
Donald Trump Jr.
Ivanka Trump
kun zhao

Long –She – Ma – Yang –Hou –Ji-Gou –Qiu –Zhu-Yuwin

analysis of
Rouche, Hurwitz, Weierstrass,
Taylor, Sobev, Yuwinzar, Cauchy conculusion,

Ex: Solve x^4 – 6z + 3 =0 in circle of |z| <1, 1 < |x| < 2,
     inner zeros

Answer:

let f(z) = -6z
    g(z) = z^4 -6z +3

on circle of |z| =1,

we see | z^4 + 3| = | Z^4 – 6z +3 - (-6z)| = | g(z) –f(z)| =4,
        |-6z| = 6 |z| =|f(z)| =6

we deduce that |z^4 +3| =4 < 6=|-6z|

which means |f(z) –g(z)| < |f(z)|

by Rouche Theory, **_g(z) and f(z) have the same number of solutions on |z| < 1,_** since $f(z) = -6z$ has only 1 zero on $|z| < 1$,

let $F_1(z) = z^4$, on $|z| = 2$,

$|g(z) - f_1(z)| = |-6z+3| = 9$ Or $15 < 16 = |z^4| = |f_1(z)|$

in short, $|g(z) - f_1(z)| < |f_1(z)|$

by roaches' theory,
$g(z)$ on $|z| = 2$ has the same zeros as $f_1(z)$, which means $g(z)$
has 4 zeros

since on $|z| = 1$
$|g(z) - f(z)| < |f(z)|$,
$|z| = 1$ implies $g(z)$ not equal to 0,
thus, $g(z)$ on $1 < |z| < 2$, has $4-1=3$ zeros

Text that Sit at Math Student Carlos Kong's Desks

1: introduction to PDES and waves for the Atmosphere and Ocean
    by Andrew Majda

2: Lectures on Analysis of Non-linear PDE Vol 4, 5
    by Jean-Yves Chemin, Fanghua Lin, Bing Zhang

Ps: by Lebesque space, the following interpolation holds as an
application of Holder inequality, $P\_1 < Q < P\_2$

$$1 / Q = Q / P\_1 + (1-Q) / P\_2$$

we have $\| f \|\_g <= |f|\_{p1} {}^{\wedge}Q + |f|\_{p2} {}^{\wedge}(1-Q)$
similar holds in Sobolev space
page 303 (zhang xiaoyi)

3:   Graduate Texts in Mathematics by wolfgang Walter

4: Partial Differential Equations (2nd edition) by Lawrence c. Evans

5: Singular Intergrals and Differentiability Properties of Functions
by Ellias Stein

6: Fubian Hanshou (p185) by Zhuang Qitai, zhang Nanyue, Shang
Yansheng, ChangXin Miao

7: Analysis (2nd editotion) by Elliott H. Lieb, Michael Loss

all day pass at 7-11 shop, after Dunkin-Donuts

75, 282, 5, 3,
Coronado Inn, 2009
Palm <-> Third Street, 500
Alameda, R. H. Dana, Adella,
Glorietta Bay Inn, 2772
Coronado Museum of History
Avenida Der Mundijay 1700
Silver De Las Arenas Strand 1800

Some Schools that seem interesting to Skylar Peng

San Diego state university
(E =mc^2)
u of Chicago
u of Texas at Austin
Taiwan Yang Ming university
u of Tennesee
northwestern university at Evanston
northeastern university at Boston
Harvard University
Princeton University
Stanford University
Shenzhen University
Sun Yat-Sen university
Jinan University
Peking University
Beijing wuzi University
Renming university
Taiwan University
Capital Normal University
South China Normal university
Fudan University
Wuhan University
shanghai Jiaotong university
Shenyang gongye daxue
Beijing Jingji University
Shandong University

惠民香港周
红心北美彭

--- Mu Naiyi (Tom Hanks)

澎湖荣荣江燕
飞飞净水杨柳

---Zhao Wu (abbey yin)

冰雨去呢要吃无
韶华好管理员修

--- Fan Dousong (Fannie Mayer)

唐朝盛世无价红
川菜好课经龙潭

---- jiao Zuohu (Jerry Brown)

莫言春风一夜小
眼肌无声龙是草

---Yan Xiaowei (Karen Pence)

书画魔官道
刘银米钱堂

--- Wang Mogao (Nancy Pelosi)

父子长江桥
母女屋山鸟

--- **Shi qi Kong que (Robin Perini)**

绥棱贵州英
爱红店魔方

---Zhu Huiqing (Maxium Zuckerburg)

普天新能源
厦门航空官

by one drop of water (yi dishui)

尼克松独立
万多福开心

by Yan Wuji (woody Guthrie)

蓝天白玉春雨无
红衣黑裙未名湖

by Tang tianzheng (Shelton Fu)

路边行人匆匆行
华山诗文行行亭

by Peng Yuewan (Amelia Wilson)

月半小夜曲
谁 **听古巨基**

by Yang Lan (Briana Blair)

C. J. Williams scores Large

Large points
high Baskets
Howard, New Year, Hampton, Resident Inn, Baymont
all smart owls
hooting above Mont. Langya,
the crowds grow tense
when Bruno Wu and Yao Ming throw a ball in a basket,
3 point go,
we hear sharp screams,

bloody pride
Ting Wu and Todd Holm art,
Tom is curious,
He wants to relax,
while dreaming of better sports of Curt Sharp, Max Barry,
the world falls sleep
little eyes pop bubbles in Paradise Branson,
Shanghai princess Abbey writes,
she seems hot with Glenn Debb, Sam Farmer, Tom Bradley

The Flash Light Sergey Brin holds

He holds a flash light
 trying hard to discover treasure
A mouse hides behind
 creaking some sweet noise,
 the man seems mindless
 blind or mute,
sitting in a vacuum for a thousand year long,
not ageing with Pat Quinn's son,
not knowing George Bush's mother,
not reading Bill Clinton's bio,
until Julio Ottino and Larry Page join the game,
giving him a Thunder Sundar Pichai,
with the game machine going on and on,
David Drummond, Chuck Reed, Eric Schmidt come
Steven Jobs, Paul Ryan, Michael Dell, Donald Trump come
James Apple, Gary Johnson, Ron sharp, Ralph Steele come

...

the man becomes awake

The anxious Ox

some monkeys never climb trees
but do stairway hoping
it feels like fine tuning a guitar string,
our heartbeats is filled with musical rhymes,
Jenny worries,
Markshen thinks aloud,
Tom and Abbey pay attention to Lilyn and Meredith,
Chris and Christina tuck Emily, Sheby, Yuri, and Jae to bed,

Audubon park is hot wired
people ride bikes,
people drum concrete floors
people give away books by Sarah Thorrick or Mark Twain,
people ignore George Eastman for a change,
if Tom Benson does not redo Gamebit prints,
Wilson Nelson and Heidi Cruz will relax,
how to get to Tagg Romney / Jim Murphy street?
ask Big Bird Mitt Romney or Elmo Markshen Hurley!1

The Envelope quote

inside anything anyone,
there is some value there,
unsent love, forgotten currency,
distant memory, foggy dreams,
let it be,
either in a wooden nickle
or in a case of backpack
I ride a rollercoaster
feel the thrill
of ups and downs
my figure prints say a story,
my pen traces "BJD10 → LAX52F" clockwise

I forgive Lucinda's persistence

Los Angeles Times

American Air delivers satisfaction,
closely to Sanya residents,
a trip circulates,
around or above ---
Beijing, Nanjing, Guangzhou, Shenzhen,
Taipei, Phoenix, Seoul, Boston, Gainsville,

who sets record on Fiji islanders?
why does Jackie Chan or Brad Pitt win Hollywood?
recall a movie by Xiaogang Feng, you Ge,
trusting intelligence of Hongjian Gao, Jian Cao, Feng Xie
we make some case better here,
keep it up, Qingxia Lin, Han Ching, David Zahniser,

Holdensville,
Grace Pickens sets up book shelves,
Fengjiao Lin, Ji Yan, Huimin Zhou, Yazhi zhao join,
Zouming Fang, Rann Wang, Melissa Galway, Sisi Chen join,
we sell wines from Great Wall footsill,
making Jennifer Feguson, Megan Barry, mike Finnegan feel
good about Kate Mather's pick on Wendy Schmidt shoe makers

Abbey Wood, a mother to Lilyn Cheekawood, Meredith Donaldwood, Markshen Atwood, Eric Greenwood, Sam Tuckerwood, Heidi Alexwood

Emily Wilson FarmHood

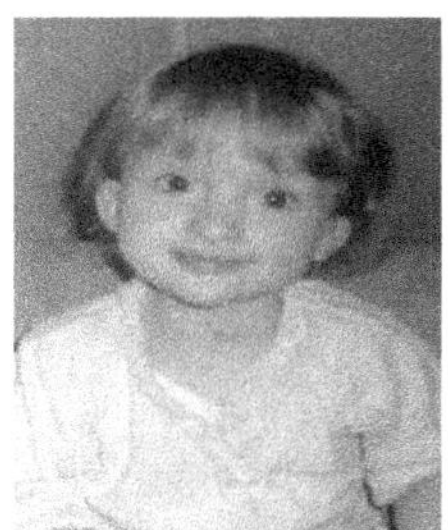

Sheby Blairmoore

Jenny Zhang, poet from this book
she has previous work published as
K. D. Hurley, Iris Chang, Ina Davis, Wilson Gremer,

Hotels and Resorts that Benny Wu & Christina Mulvane enjoy

Howard Hotel, Taipei
Oaktree, Livonia
Crownze, Atlanta
La Quinta, Denton
Resident Inn, Pullman
Comfort, Manchester
4 Point by Sheraton, Little Rock
Extended Stay America, Nashville
Oread, Lawrence
Staybridge, Rochester of New York
Dylan, San Francisco
Jinlong Tan, Beijing
New Year Hotel, Shenzhen
Gaslamp hotel, San Diego
Hampton, Guangzhou
Kaifeng hotel, Guangzhou
Lucky Hotel, Guangzhou
Haocai hotel, Guangzhou
Vanugh Hotel, Guangzhou
Hyatt Place, Tulsa
Hotel 6, Fort Worth
Regional Days Inn, Altus
Clarion, Elk city
Micro Hotel, Arkansas
Holiday Inn, Chicago

James Inn, Chicago
Courtyard, North Brook
Alexia Inn, Nashville
 Motel 8, Wichita
Holiday Inn, Lebanon,
 Red Roof Inn, Kansas City,
 Ramanda Inn, Norman
Jinjiangzhixin "Ji", Shanghai
Ziyu hotel, Beijing
Jingshi Hotel, Beijing
Hotel Indigo, New Orleans
Hampton, New Orleans
Wyhdam, Chelsea of New York
Fairfield Inn, Boston
 Homewood, Princeton
 Sonesta, Princeton
 AmericaInn, Madison
 Baymont, Des Moise
 Sleep Inn, Fayetteville
 Days Inn, Dallas
 Best Western hotel, Jefferson City
 Cambridge university hotel, London
 Chung Ang University hotel, South korea
 Academia Sinica hotel, Taipei
 Tunghai University hotel,   Taichung

Oyster, Napoleon road, New Orleans, LA

Luyu fish hot pot, Happy Valley,
Guangzhou famous dish....
above, Bailey Hendrickson, Mary Clancy,
not pictured, Susan Wojcincki, Mary Fisher
Benny Wu, Terry Murphy, Loraine Chan

Who dares invade space in Yahoo Merissa Mayer's home?

sample list, not to be told as offensive

忧康慧
万仁辉
霍小苹
董柏青
吴然超
杜先能
黄德宽
何家庆
别马马
顺德佬
梅世雄
梅兰芳
梅<u>常伟</u>
韩文强
韩文嘉
盛佳婉
孔水晶
任晓明
吴中伟

焦新
莫诗浦
张晨
白云怡
杜毅
陈毅
杜天奇
沈德永
严文静
颜文俊
马建忠
谢华
刘彦木
张悦
何新伟
钱济荣
戚森伟
朱兴良
邓仕军
施利君
鞠倩蔚
林冲
高以翔
吴胜
链战
周劲松

周锦寿
季水河
彭国甫
胡耀
关汉卿
彭传新
彭传会
颜佳华
颜佳
颜霁
黄维德
科迪
洞庭湖
李仲谋
徐一鸣
洪锦标
秋瑾
黄四清
黄思勤
吴子良
汤唯
冯晓颖
杨澜
杨婉芳
芳华
汤新颖

柳颖
柳岩
陈独秀
程佩斯
朱时茂
朱青阳
闫永春
严咏春
严中华
颜中华
燕飞
延吉
谭小艳
王志文
葛优
成立
成勇
成功
钟声
钟无艳
钟南平
何现龙
钟铜
冯小刚
冯翠珊
冯德全
尹建莉

Quote of 连战 (Thomas Zhan)

进步*前瞻*

最求卓越

Progress Way Ahead

Seek Jolly Points Farrest

Sun Yat-Sen University in Taiwan

Forgive yuan juanmin,
Forgive ching han,
Get to know Jiang Yuheng,
Get to know Lin Lichi,
Listen to Lin Yilian,
Listen to Joel Yung,
Read Chiong Yao,
Read Jiao Fuyun,
Recall Ye Jianying,
Recall zhang Wei,
we become strong,
Stronger than wu wenjun, shen jie, and huo shengjing

Huanan Shifan next to Jinan University

Tian Bingxian,
Xun Guanliang,
Zhong Kaijie,
Tang Wei,
Wu Aimei,
Fan Meihua,

famous stars hang themselves high,
higher than John Hancock skyline,
Don't you ever wonder,
Poet Bai Juyi,
Poet Yan Jing Ge,
Poet Yi Lunjing,
Poet Wang Min.
Poet Peng Chuanxian,

how about poet He zhaokuang?
how about poet Zhu Daihong?
how about Gao Xiaomin?
how about poet Yan Ju Er?

according to Yang Lan, Bruno Wu, we love poems by Juji Gu

Sam Walton's Walgreen and Shell

American gas is odd,
Larry shell or Larry gosney,
Jayne Kim or Chelsea Kim,
all serve, all secure,
State Farm, Geico, Safeco,
howard Johnson does some humor,
adding juice to our poetry table,
Milton latter, Hilton howard, Richard allen,
Stanley Thomas, Ted cruz, sarah constantin,
we search in a church,
seeing patricia gay, the mother to Don Belt,
she adores daughter Wang Ai Qun,
who seems refuses to quit writing,
alan Adophson is an uncle to Heidi Cruz,
amy wong, Sophia Trump, mimi Schapiro,
they write from Illinois,
they echo Emily Dickinson,
they agree to give aya Wilson's poems a go

Xavier University and Yu Bingyu, He Dajie, Yan Guohua

it costs
Alan Yu
to know
a relative
Kathryn Drexel,
if Winn v Dixie,
never appears, Wu Wenhui,
she invites zhao Yun, and Sun quan to the party,
Why Walmart?
Why Epcot?
Why rouses?
according to Terry Murphy,
Audie murphy and Pamela murphy
could linger behind Todd Holm and Tipper Gore,
that easy mark bookmarks shine,
in Rainbow colors,
revealing a century history to budding readers

a cloud of smoking heads

lu jian, bu jing, zhan xinzhi, xu changing, su guifu,
liu chongwen, huo shengjing, he zhengyu, tan bo,
lin yilian, pan bingbing, fan bingbing, zhao wei,
wu yuanqing, cao lihua, zhou yan, tao qiang, feng jiqiang,
xiong xiangming, wang dehua, zhu xiaofeng, peng danping,
zhou ningning, zhou tao, li shuangjiang, li guyi, zhang ye,
guan mucun, deng lijun, Teresa teng, meng lijun, han zhe
ameliawilson, abbey wood, robin Perini, Rachel coterrill,
kandare blake, andy Wilson, Bristol frankwood, Cynthia
brown, Jessica yen, tina wu, wavely wang, Richard yang,

blooming self-esteem under Brian Sweeney

far at southeast
near Qiantang river,
a magpie bridge paves a way
that is between ox boy and weaving lady,
the twin boys are made
the neighborhood is cheered
queen Walrus and princess Stephanie
both good and aggressive,
setting a boat on sailing,
ox-tiger relation,
chick-sheep curiosity,
lovely children dance ballet
Igor Hope Montuwa place more Hong Kong dim sum there,
what a Kwuang Tong happy valley
we use subway to arrive at Wanlin square,
buy a book by zhang Ailing, and by Yan Geling

Call Me Mosaic Bookstore

after huang xiaoming and wu aihong leave,
we chew hard,
see the baby face from Li Haoran, Gong Xianghong,
tough mind becomes softer

who is that child?
Dou Yi, Guan Yu, Wu Tiejian, Emily Quinn?
some street news run hot,
Guanzhou Daily promote poetry groups,

Nanyang, Sigapore,
Aimer / Abby/ New Look / Amelia / Sheyi stand firm,
Qtools / Chris / LuYu Fish / Eric / Jill all cute,
how about read a "Huashi daily"?

Jenny and Benny walk around,
paying more attention to Lily, SpiceBox, LAVA, Edenus,
they wish that books from Joy Evelyn can help
a favorite stop, which is "Call Me Mosaic Coffee" stop

Shi xiaojun's Motovation in Writing

Lin Yan,
Melania Trump,
Ziqi Wang,
Moling Ye,
Yiwei Xie,
Shuqiong Yi,
Dou Lan,
Hongyan Yin,
Ying Niu
Tom L. Wu,
Lanfeng Yu

..

a group,
a crowd,
a voice,
a poem,
a story,
all sound and clear
they figure out a way to reach out
small pool of waves does make Ningxia gouqi more fame
Brenda sheng, Aaron Hendrickson, P. F. Clancy, all bright

Quote of "Liang Shan Gong Fu" teahouse

Nothing

is

more

Fabulous

than

Family

Notable Writers /authors from Stockholm, Sweden

duan wenjing, cheng ying, lin hai, wang qi, shi cheng,
xu liang, han xun, wu shijian, wu shiyun, ding xue er, tang xi,
zhao bo, Zhuang nu, dong yanyi, fu xia, kong qiangfeng, yan ji,
wang bingbing, ya nida, han cai, yang jiahui, jiao kou, niu ying,
li juan, ding xiaohui, yao li, guo jie, tong shuqian, ox song, fred
perry, lily brown, zheng hong, yi shu, jing rong, shen zeyi,
chang lang, shiqi gongqiao, yi wenjuan, wenchang guan,
wenchong , nian zhan, xiao bei, leide, tan cun, shiban qiao,
Kunming hu, wanshou shan, zhongguo jiaoyu bao, Huangpu
dadao, ying bing, wu aimei, yan simei, peng zhongqiang, chai lu
dong qing, dong yi, dong fang, chen lan, li hongbing, hu qiao,
sheng wu, gong xiao, xie xiaodong, sun jianfei, liu ying, san mao

liu jie, he zhaokuang, shen miao, wang wei, wang ying, yan ji,
zhang xinjun, zhao jing, zhao xin, peng xin, zhou feng, shen jia,
Mikaela Shiffrin, Jamie dimon, shi futian, dara khosrowshahi,
bob gill, robin li, zhiyuan yang, yongcui yan, fusheng peng,
meihua peng, yuanzhen peng, yuanxi peng, chenlin yang,
lan yang, yongqi liang, youju cheng, qunzhi yang, jing qiu

Quote of He Zhaokuang (baidu.com 何兆武, 何昭匡力)

传者泰兴，知之无境

Pastors extend richness to enrich
knowledge base braids infinity

Wavely Trump 's pick on
award winning individuals
under National Science Foundation of China , Siyuan lab

Yin Hongyan
Cui Ni
Pang Qichang
Hu Cuiying
Deng youjin
Liu Pengyi
Xie Weiguang
chen xianzhou
yan jichi
peng wenping
wu qixin
sheng kesu
fan xudong
yang jidong
chen zhe
sun jinan
he yousheng
Frieder Seible
nie zhenghua
lai zhenghuan
ning zhihua
li linyan
hong jingquan
wang yu
tang zhengfang
zheng dongqing
yin hao
xu lanfang
liu qian
qiu tian
zhou huaqi

Haocai, Chongqing malla spicy food

Hao Cai,
Chongqing Mala,
Tang xiaomian

Food fancy
li xuan, fan min,
proceeding li haoran, li qingzhao

wu aihong, fan yunqing,
wu jialiang, zhang wangying,
all seem fine with fan bowen, wu sheng, tom ku, steven tucker,

if Barron Trump, Eric Trump, and Donald Trump Jr. won't mind
we could remain high at Florida keys,
drinking white Moutai wine

Mo's
Starbuck's
Jingzhou, Dian Mofang, Aape, they come from Polly Rao

stay cool,
says Aime wood,
which is why Eric Barton, Brandon Pence, Barbara Perkins win

Merry Christmas from Hampton Inn

Merry Christmas in March 19, 2018

What does the Christmas tree see  ?

Eric and aime wood,
abbey and Thomas,
William and Linda,
Jeff and Mackenzie,
Bill William and Tanya
Brad and Kimberly
George and Laura
Abigail and Mark
Donald and Melania
Barack and Michelle
Morton and Mimi
Joseph and Martha
Michael and susan
Burns and Ann
Larry and Lucinda
Sundar and Anjali
Tim and Jeannette
Andy and Amelia
Stephan and Kathleen
Paula and Garad
Mary and Vickie
Audie and Pamela
Bruce and Megan
Phillip and Sophia
Julio and Alicia
Amy and Steven

A map of Shelley Moore district

food street   Lucky holiday hotel
  |
  |
starbucks coffee   Happy Sun mall
  |
  |
 Bing sheng Food

                                        IFC

Sun Yat-Sen university

          Pearl River   --→

    |
  |
    |

Kaifeng hotel,   Canton Tower

Liangxiang University products (Francesco Hanoi)

wu yu-tai tea
Sinopec gas
Doutai yu food
wedomei bakery
Jiajia fu shopping
tian jiao noodles
fei yan art school
super 8 hotel
yang sheng chan ting food
dongyang Zhuang dasha
great leap beer
yijie store
peng yuan hospital
yan tang milk
shu hua milk
Kentucky chicken wings and mushed potatoes
Dayingya Art
Beijing Gongshang University
Changsha Tiedao University
Si Guo Lajiao noodle house

Baishiqiaonan

a railway/subway stop,

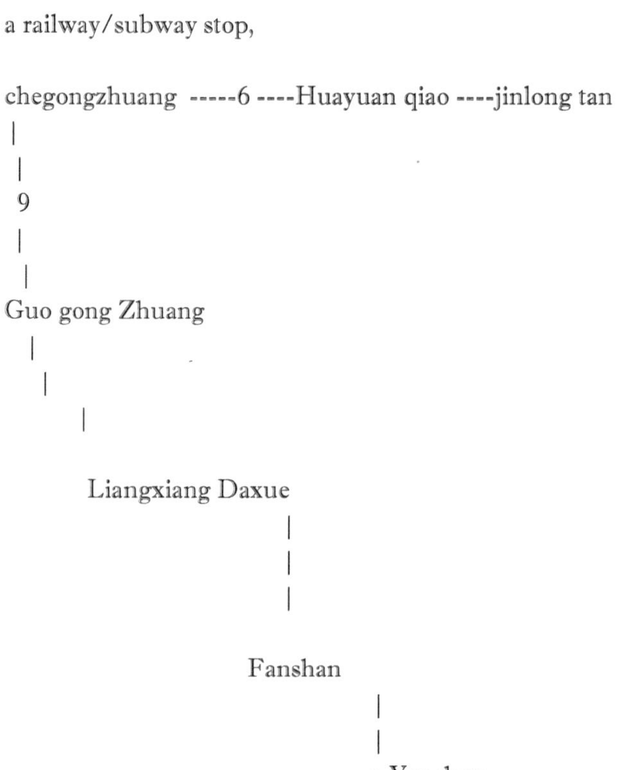

a family root tree

Wu Suo xian   <   >   Ning xia
     |
     |
   Wu Han < > Wang Yuhe
     |
     |
   Wu Huilong   < > Zhang sheng
     |
     |
  Wu Ai E   <   > Fan Xiaoyu
   |
   |
Fan Botang < > Wang Ning
  |
|
   Wang Yanxuan < > Li Peng
   |
|
    Li Bing < > Zhou Kaiming
     |
     |

   Li Keqiang (Robin Li)

Beijing international airport arrivals

赫尔辛基 Helsinki
迪拜   Dubai
台北 Taipei
东京羽田 Tokyo Haneda
罗马   Rome
香港 Hong Kong
多哈 Duoha
札幌 Sapporo
伦敦 London
旧金山   San Francisco
釜山 Busan
大阪 Osaka
冲绳 Okinana
首尔 仁川 Seoul Incheon
芝加哥 Chicago
西雅图 Seattle
达拉斯 Dallas
丹佛 Denver
北京 Peking
无锡 wushen
曼谷 Bankok

Friendly Service

at Shangri hotel,
Dong yongmei,
zhang Xinhe,
Luo Haijing,
Wang Haitang,
they clean rooms

stock rooms
shanxi tv
Nongfu spring water bottles,
things become better
if a dream is sweet
and a service is exceptional

Dong Yongmei changes the bed sheets,
she waves a cloud of cotton cloth
placing confidence in Wu Chunfeng's mother,
who happens to choose to sit,
read a good mind
and add American Safeguard soap to figuretips of Yongmei zhang

Capital Normal University Records

焰灵姬, a good colleague
赵京利, a good student
朱信萍, a distant dream
姚飞安, a close researcher
酒齐源, a mixed wine
威廉姆. 志尔摩 William p. Ziemer
        a great springer-verlag wdf
 徐志摩   a handsome poet
 严歌苓 a serious writer, Feng xiaogang has a movie on her work
J. H. Ewing, F. W. Genring, P. R. Hulmos
 weekly differnential function in Sobelev space
程丙硕, Zhouguan Caoshi cashier
索峰, a chairman for cisco
马云, a co-founder from Alibaba
 颜金歌, a startup for Thursday Poets Rally free verse (1/14/2010)
杨澜, co-founder for 杨澜访谈录, Beijing Weishi Television Inc.
尼泊尔 . 彭, Morning Pen, or Nepal Marywood, initializer to *Jingle
Poety @ Olive Garden Poetry Picnic (9/10/2011 - 9/10/2018, 7yrs)*
查斯特 . **勃肯鞋**, Charlotte Birkenstock, a charming shoe retailer
who also runs New Look clothing, amelia hair product, abbey carpet,
google watch, fitbit rubber band

special thanks go to

Xie Liutang, zheng Xiaoxin, Ren xiaoxia, zhang Zifei, miao changxin,
Jiu quansen, Peng chuanhui, Zhao weihua, Jie yan, xie yan, zhen lizhi,
Cao Yi, Tang Hexiang, Wang Daxue, Rao Mingrong, Li Jingnuo,
Yan Lixing, Yang Jianlin, Li Xuejian, Jia Yongquan, zhao baoxiu,
Guo xiao, bi Xiaoyang, Yang Lan , Wu zheng, Wei Jijun, Yu Junjian,
Liu qi, Liu Qian, Liu Shihe, Wang Xuesong, Xun Guanliang, dong Boqing,
Bing sheng, Wang Xuesong, Wang Guiqiang, Yan Siqi, Yan Simei,
Ye shaolin, Shu Tong, Li Xiu cheng, Li Xiachen, Huo Xiaoping,
Liu Yang, Xi Mingze, Peng Lijuan, Xu Zhongxun, Du Jingfang,
Ding Xiaojun, Wu Yutai, Xie Yaohuan, Lu Riying, Na Ying, Gao Yan,
Song Zuying, Chen He, Yu He, Zhang Hong, Su Hui, Tu Jun, etc.
Sun Honglan, xiao Tian, Yuan Huiqing, Li Shengsu, Li Hongtu,

Mao Dun, Lao She, Cao xueqing, wu Yiquan, Tang tingyan, zhu ning,
Feng xiaogang, Lin qingxia, Guan jinghua, Li Yanhui, hu Jintao,Yang
geng, gu juji, liang yongqi, meng shenglan, chi peicheng, larry page,
wang zhao zhao, yan xieqi, xie yingchong, liu ji, ying pingshu, lisa rowe,
gong minghong, lin qingxuan, he zhaokuang, ying li, quzinkie Scammon,
Tsai Ing-wen, Chen Shuibian, Wanda Coven, Mark Twain, Jane Mendelsoh,
Timothy Snyder, Simon Sineka, Samantha Ferns, He Guoping, joy huang,
Mary chapman, Steadman Upham, duane l. Wilson, Mary Clancy, tom jaco
Uwe Gordon, Phil bolsta, Wilson Gremer, joseph Singer, huang wenfan,
 John Kerry, joe Biden, Jill biden, Michael Pence, Yan anzhi, an Na, na ying,
scott Jackson, amelia Wilson, Milton latter, Hilton howard, Kim nelson
sarah parish, wen yiduo, Ban ki-moon, Sze Ping lo, Cheyenne murphy

www.ingramcontent.com/pod-product-compliance
Lightning Source LLC
Chambersburg PA
CBHW051908250726
48659CB00002B/548